Adult Coloring Book

Therapeutic Effect

Andrea T. Cross

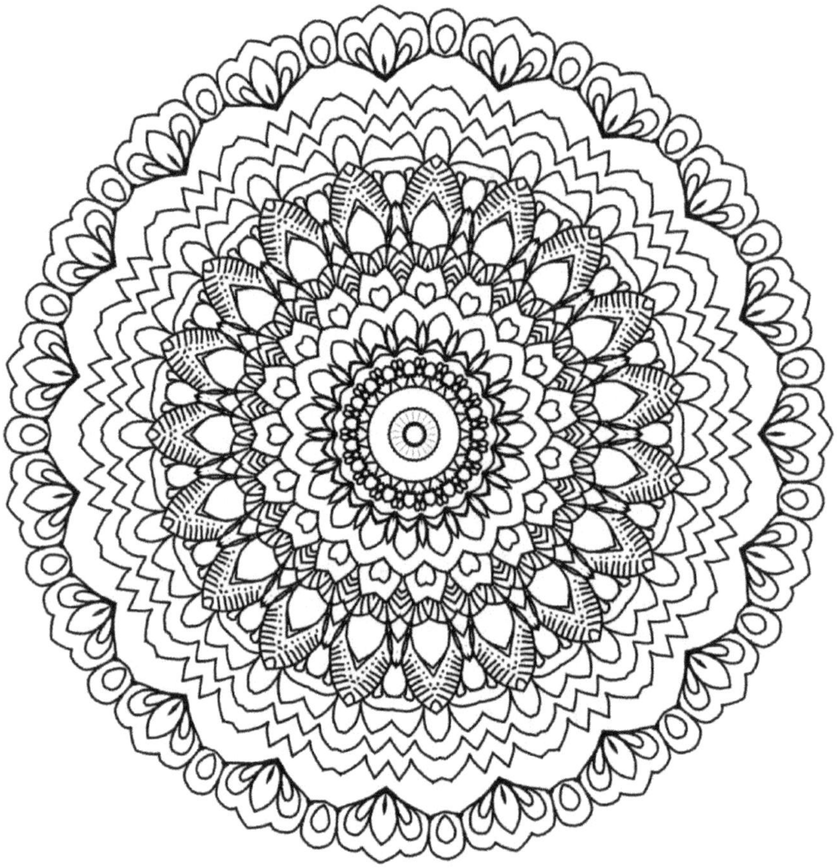

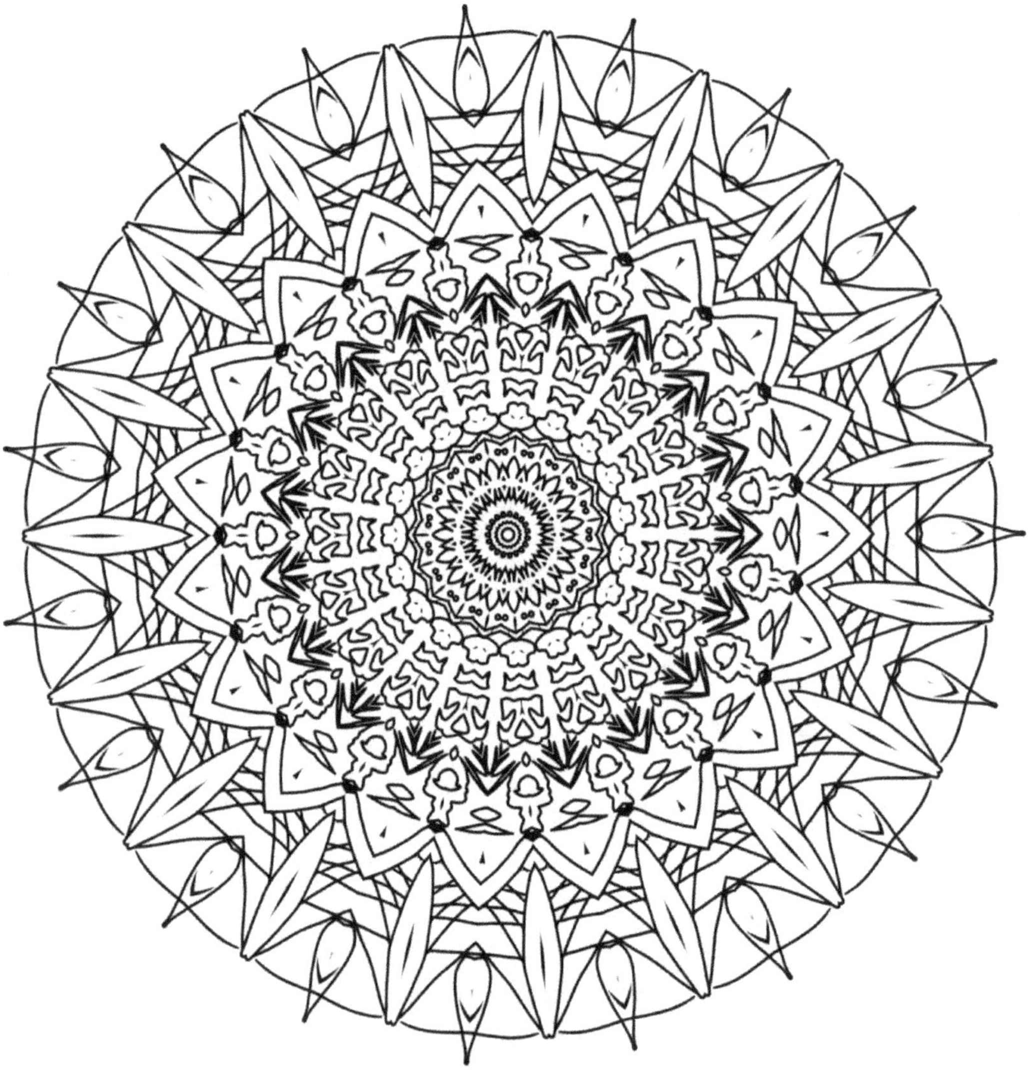

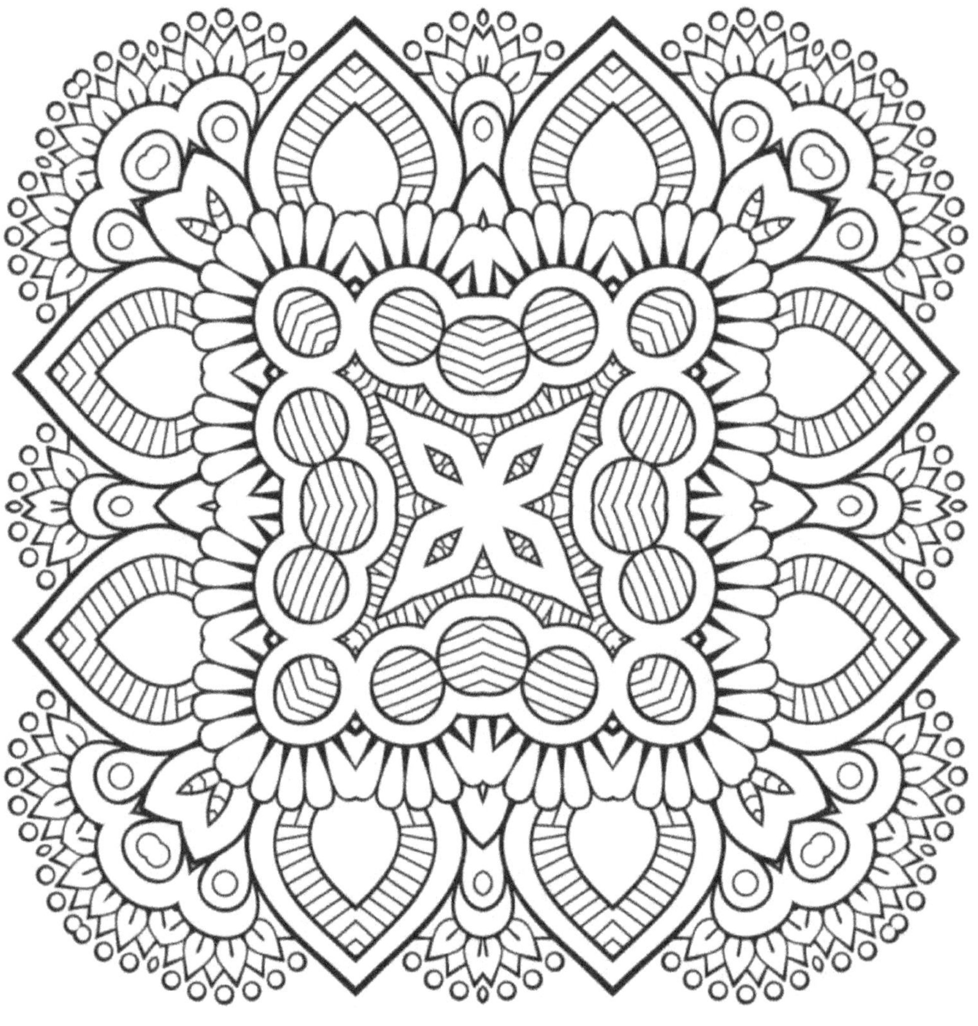

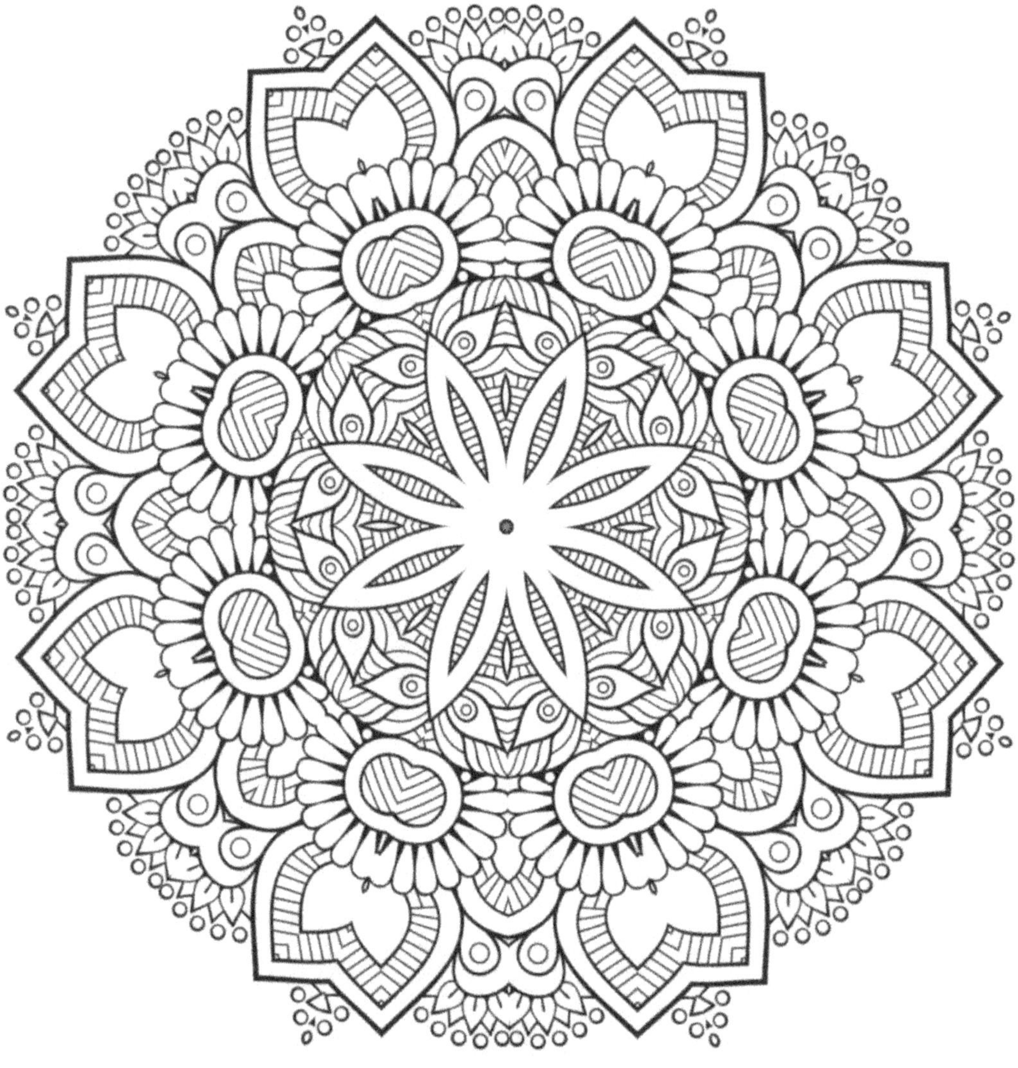

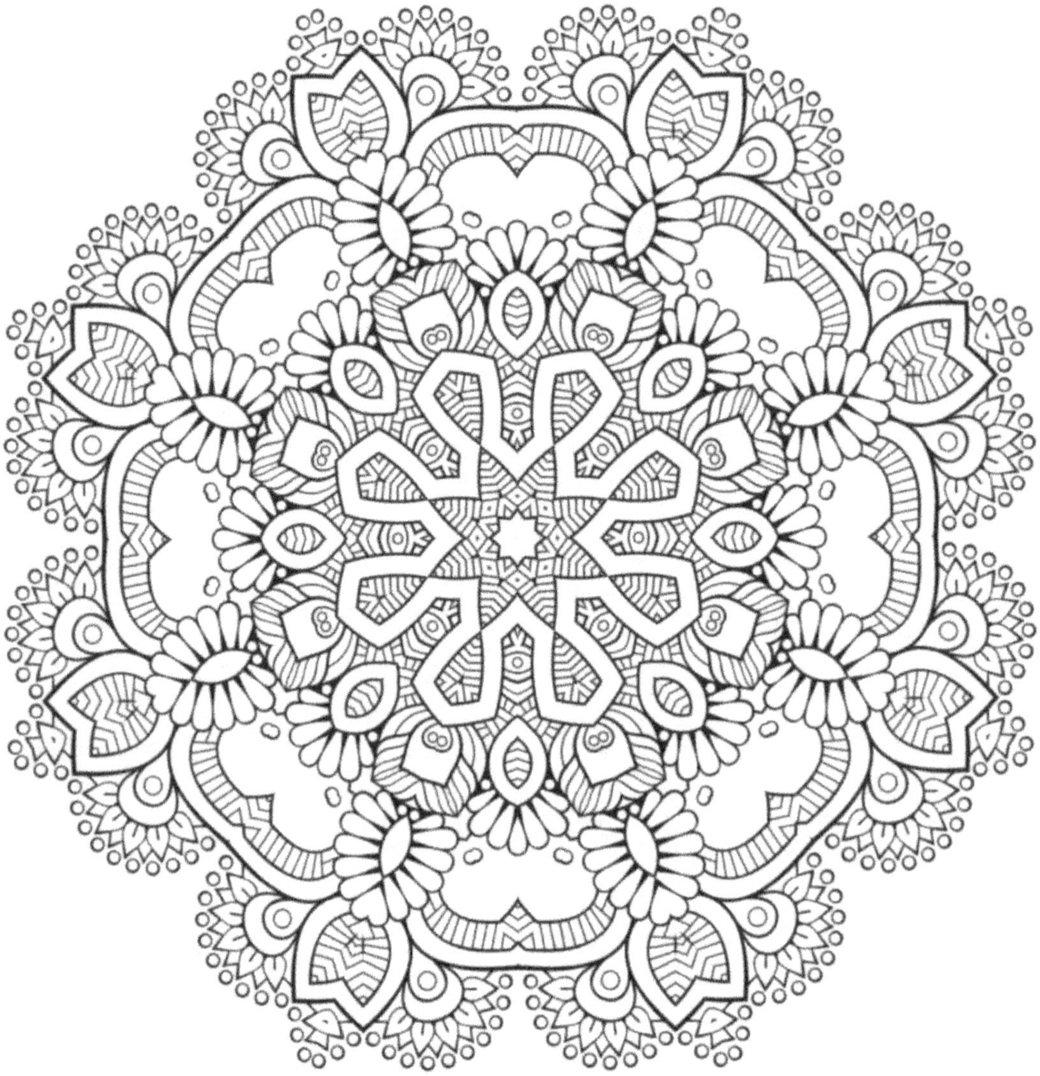

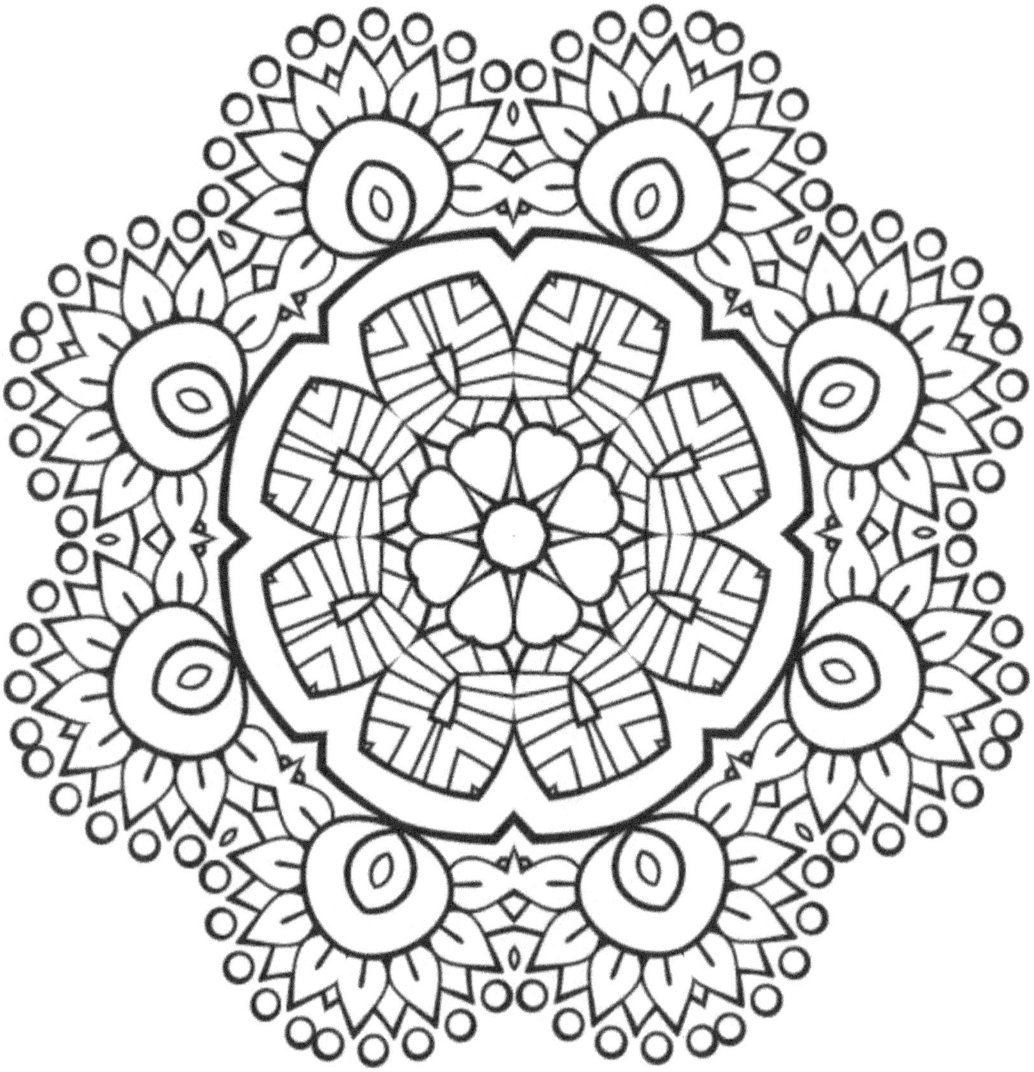

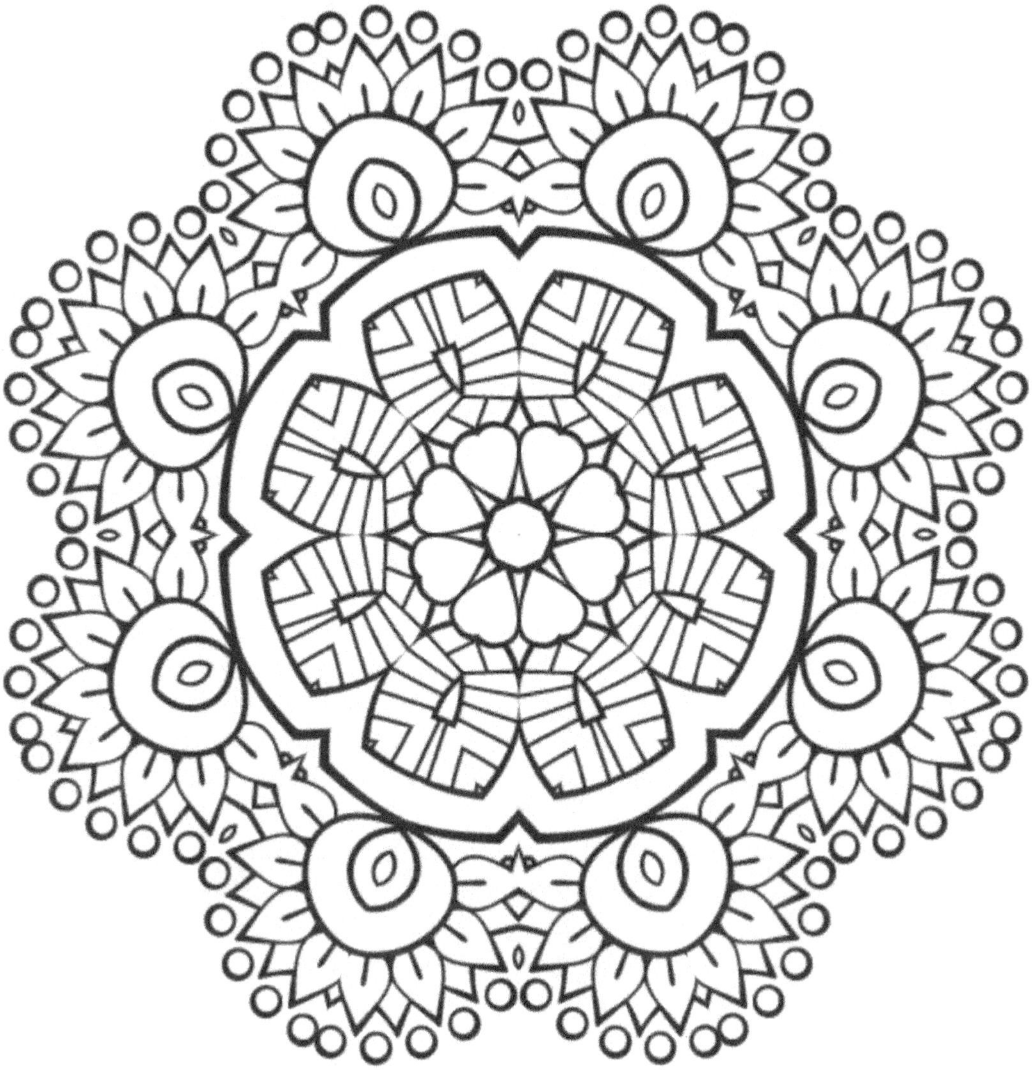

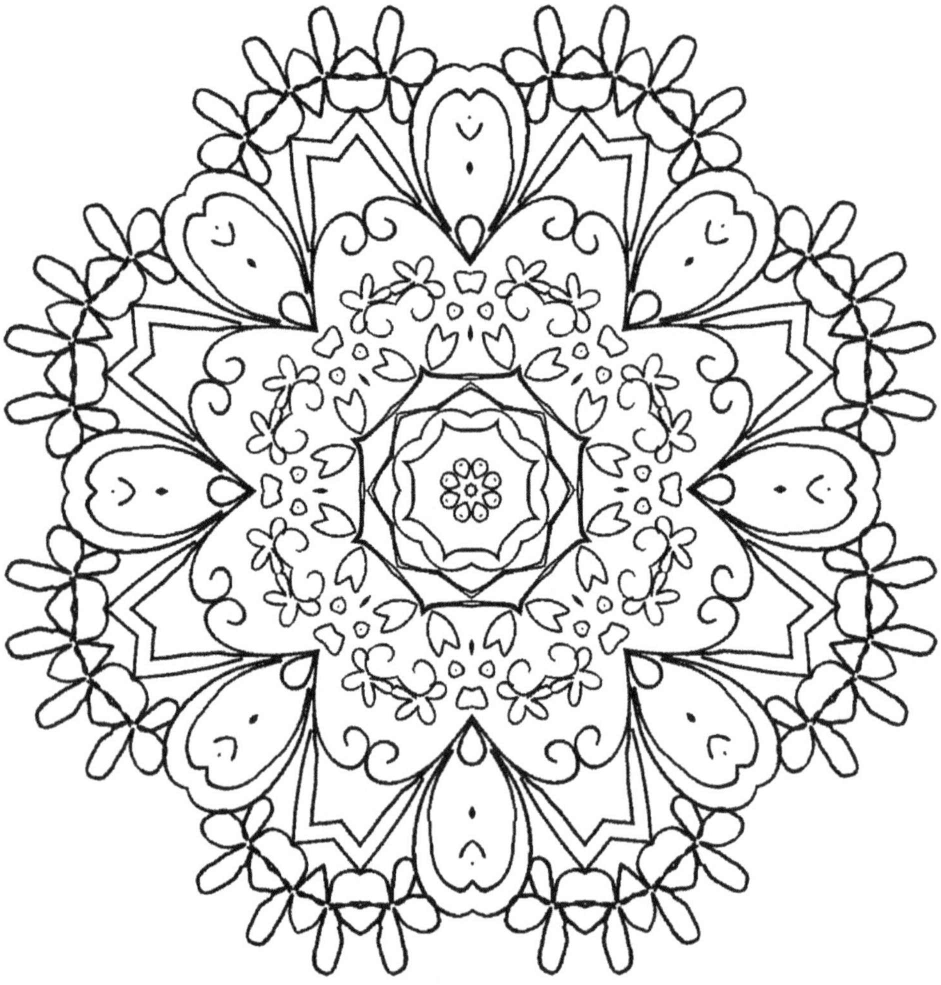

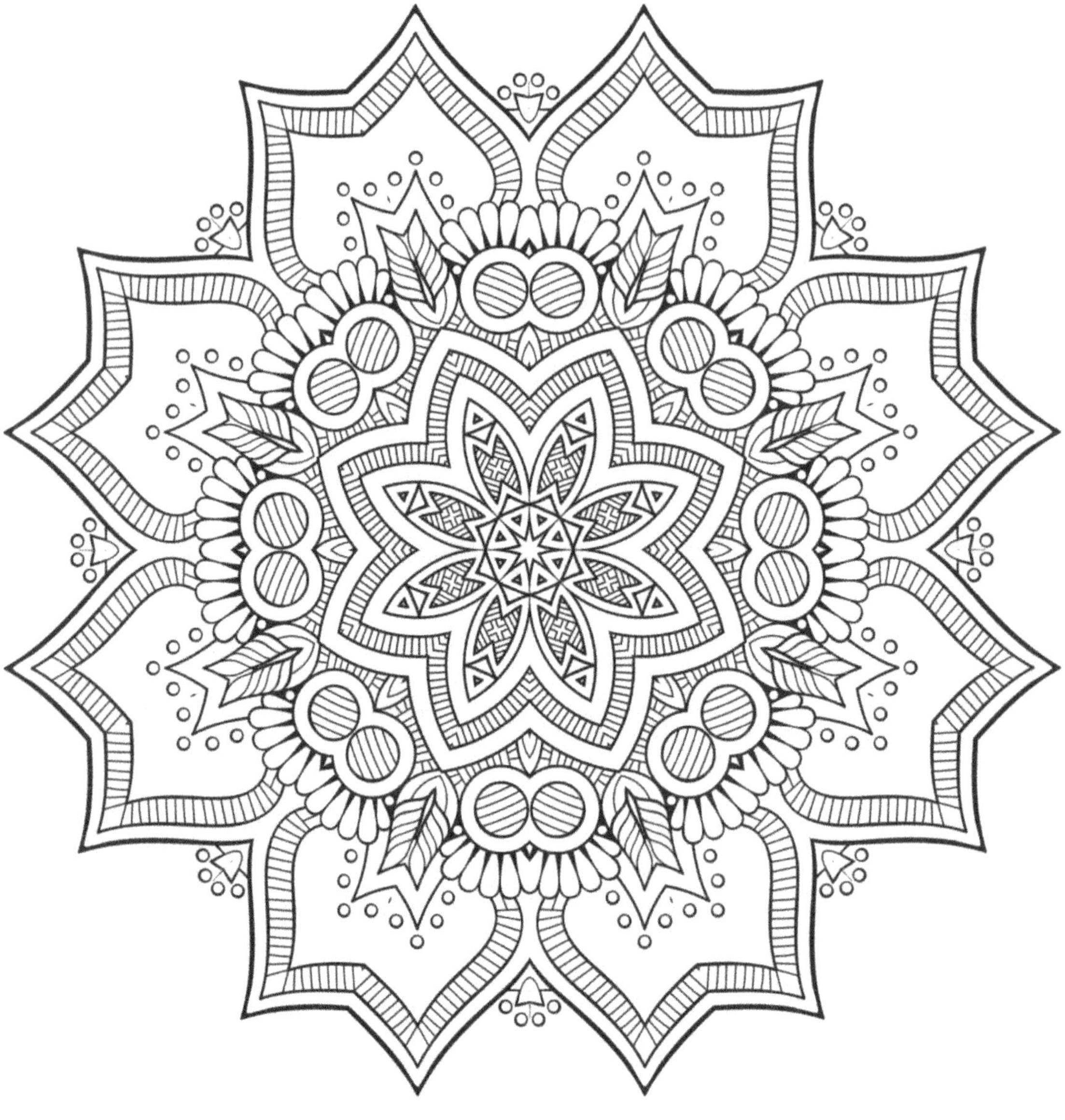

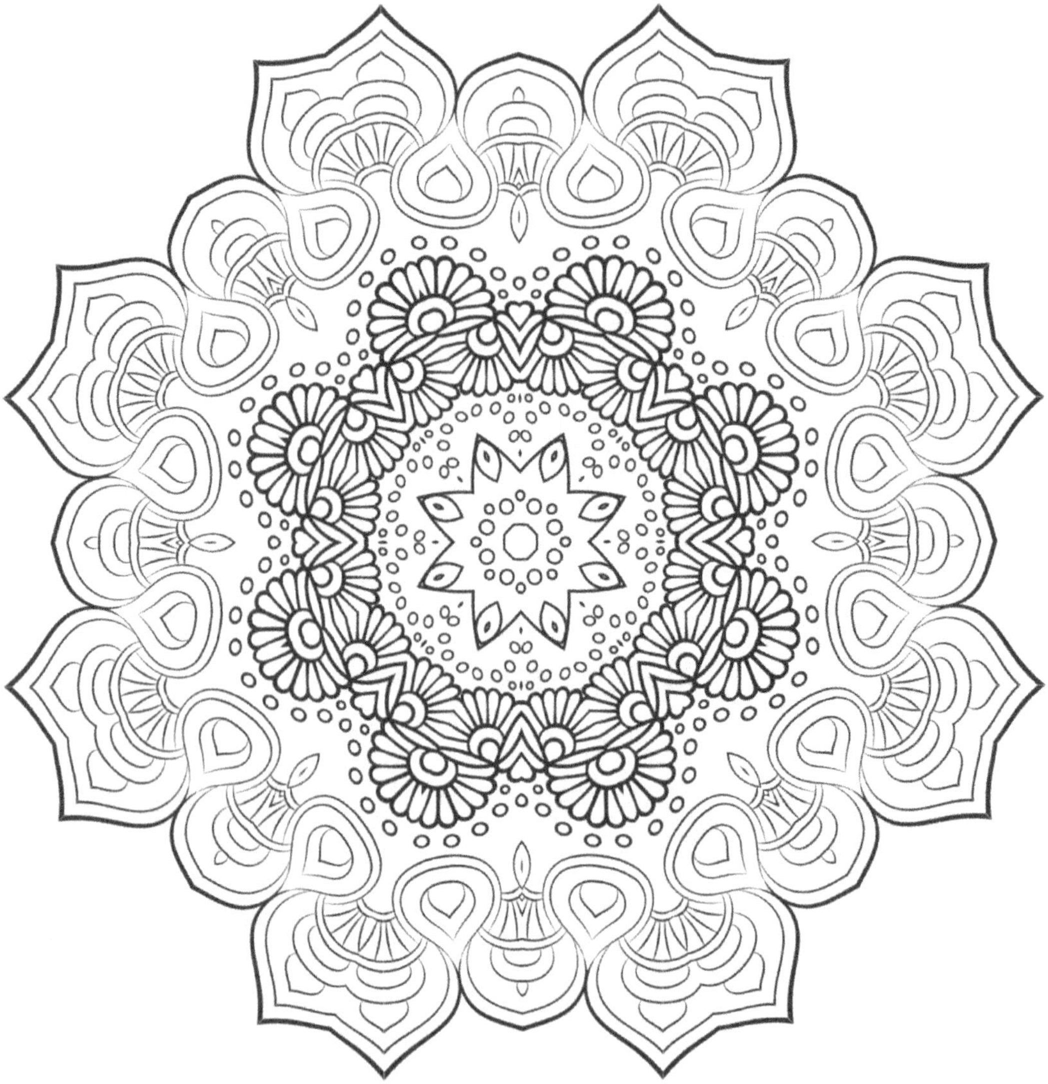

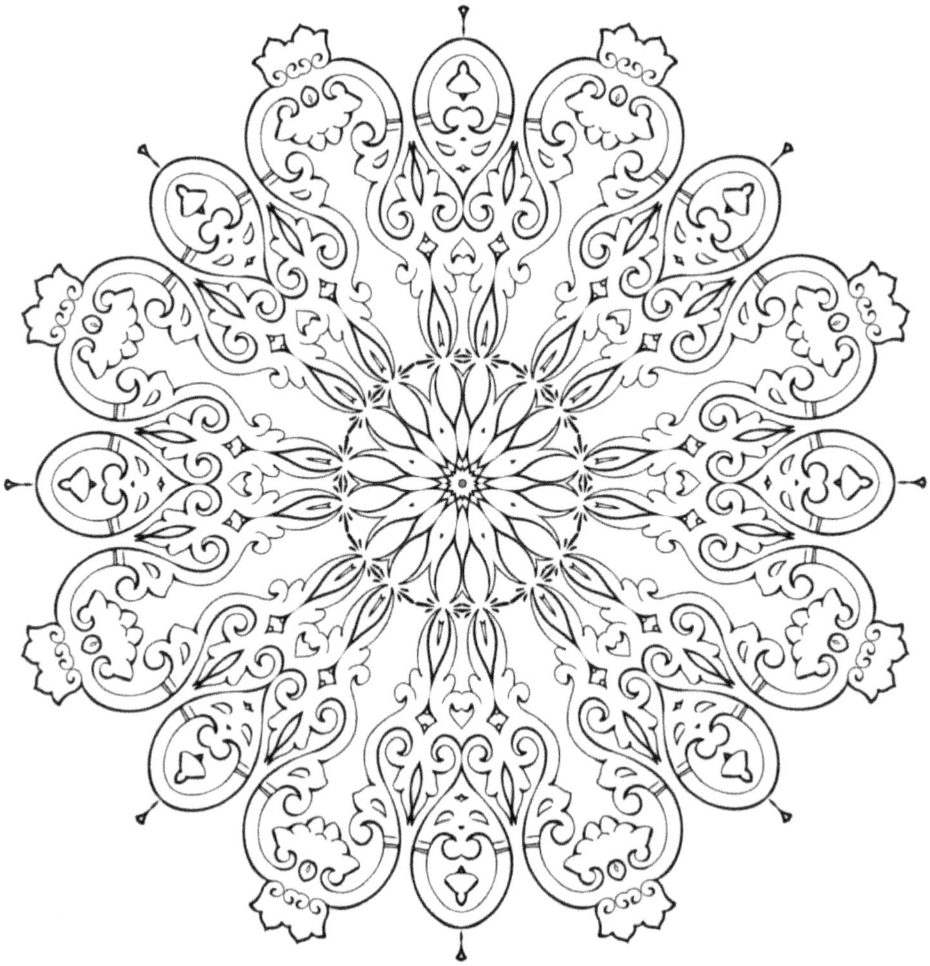

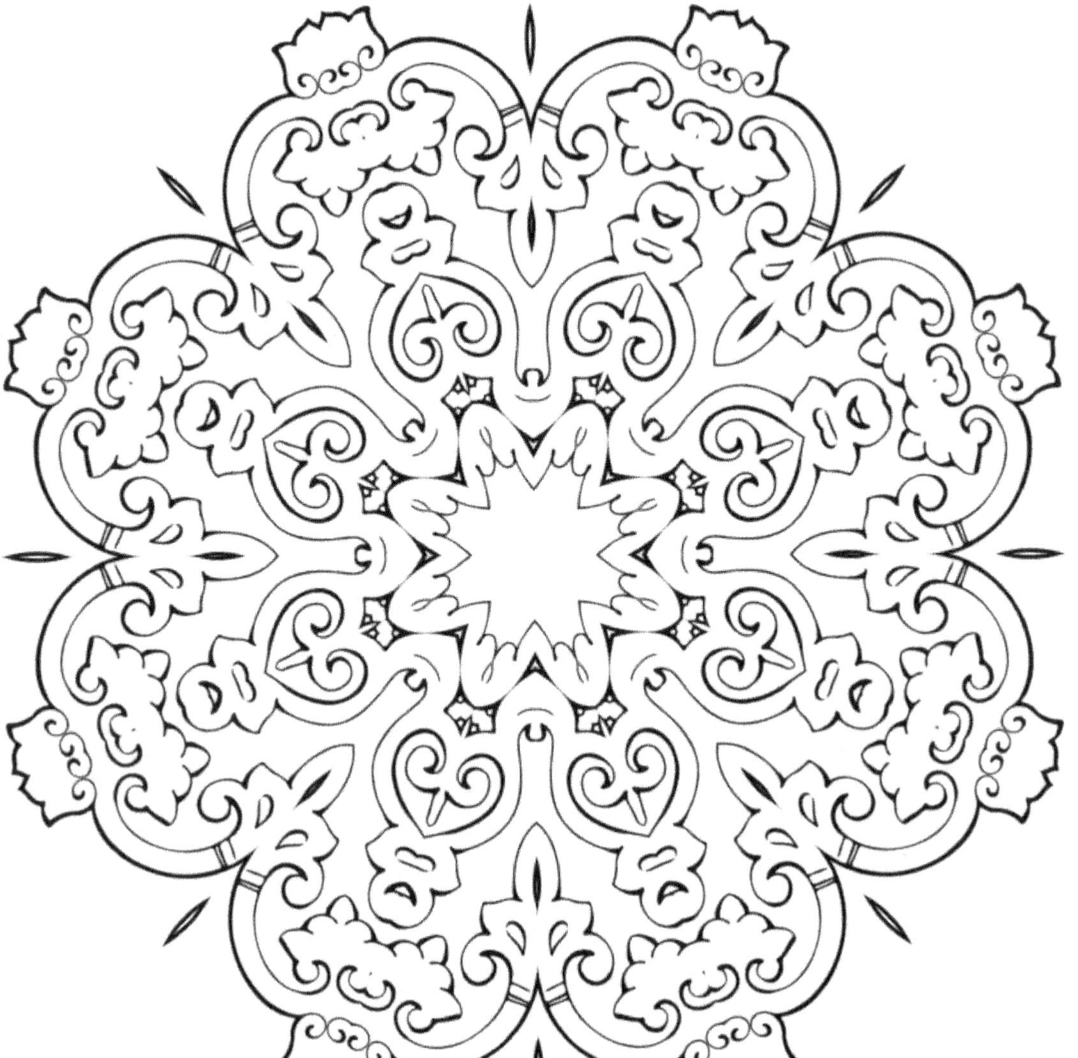

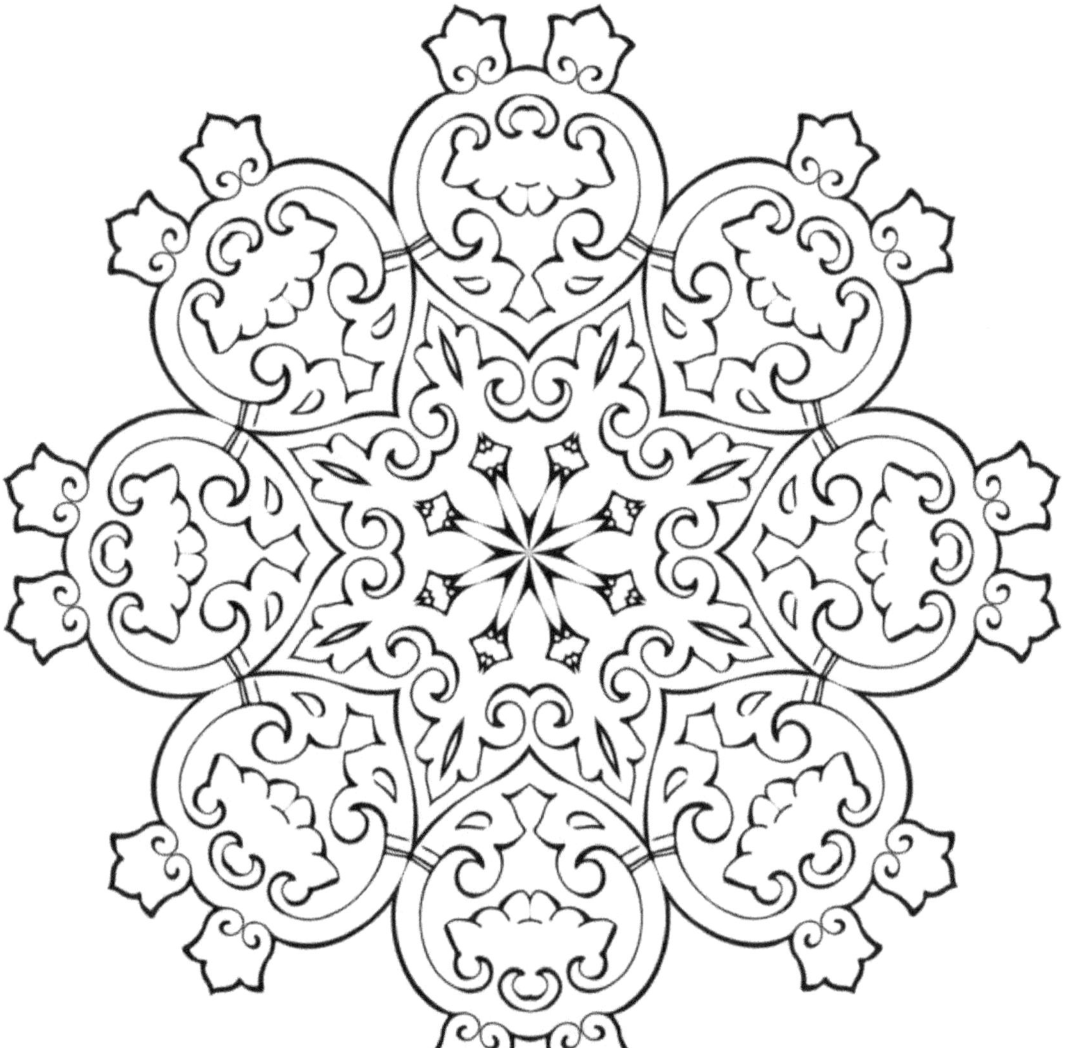

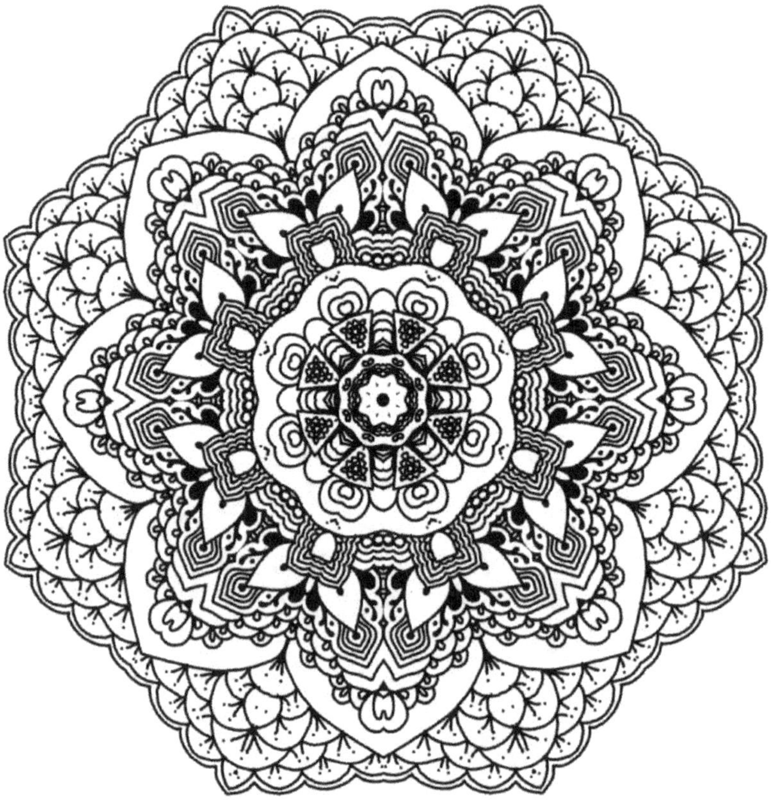

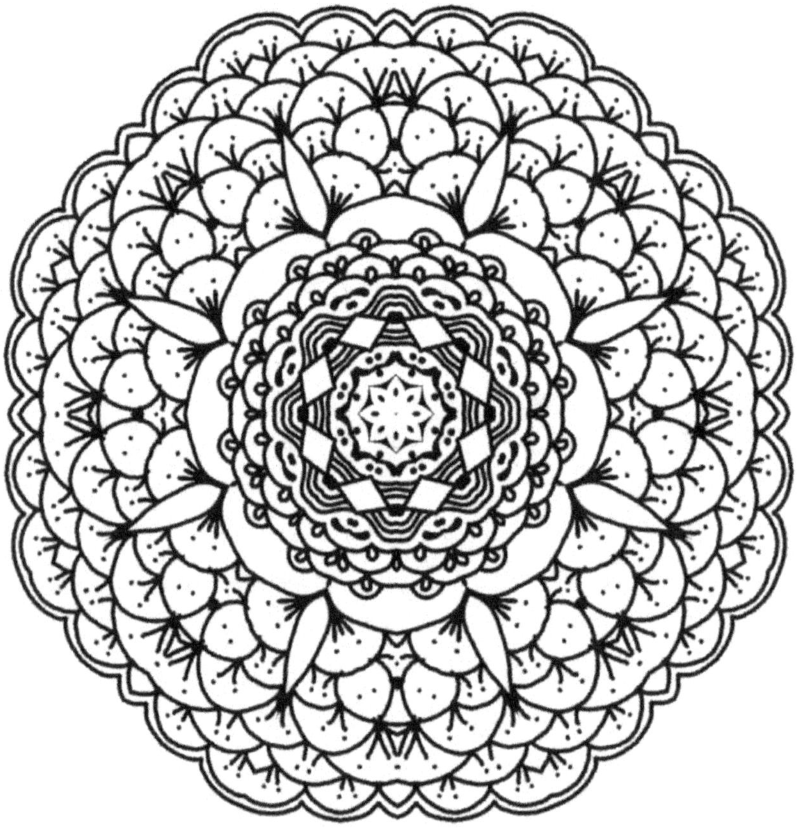

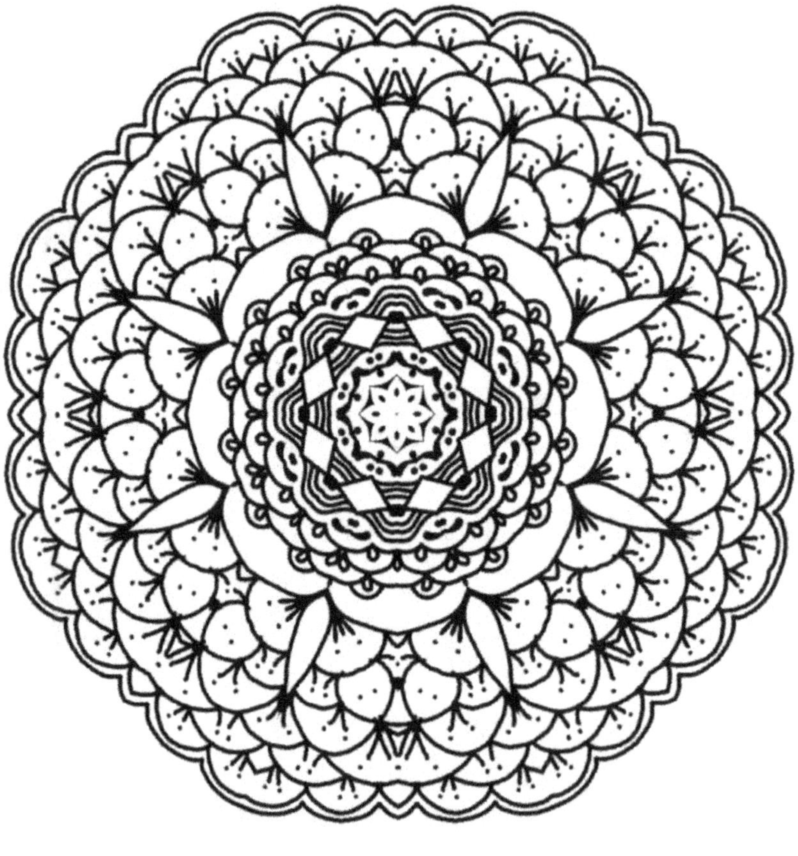

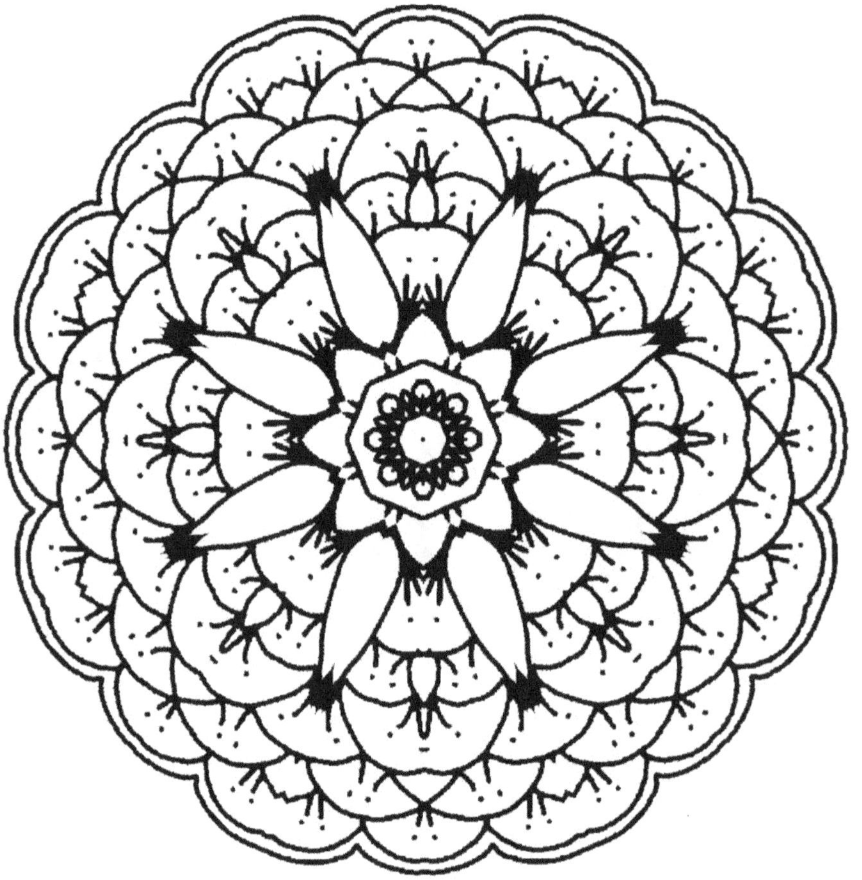

www.ingramcontent.com/pod-product-compliance
Lightning Source LLC
Chambersburg PA
CBHW081024170526
45158CB00010B/3153
* 9 7 8 1 0 8 9 9 4 1 0 8 8 *